Beautiful Girl

Written by Ciara Ijames

Illustrated by Anak Bulu

Beautiful Girl
Published by CI Publishing Group.
Copyright © 2022 Ciara Ijames.

All rights reserved. No part of this book may be used or reproduced in any manner or by any electronic or mechanical means whatsoever without written permission except in the case of brief quotations embodied in critical articles and reviews.

Printed in the United States of America

For information:
CI Publishing Group
P.O. Box 13525
Columbus, OH 43213

BISAC: JUVENILE NONFICTION / Girls & Women

ISBN-13: 978-1087910871
ISBN-10: 1087910871

All girls are beautiful

Beautiful Girl

What do you see?

I see beauty inside of me.

Beautiful Girl

What do you say?

I say beautiful things every day.

NICE

AMAZING

KIND

PLEASE

THANK YOU

LOVE

SMART

Beautiful Girl

What do you do?

I do beautiful things too.

Beautiful Girl

Where does beauty begin?

Beauty begins within!

Beautiful Girl

Who are you?

I AM A BEAUTIFUL GIRL!

Beautiful Girl
Statements

All girls are beautiful.

I see beauty inside of me.

I say beautiful things.

I do beautiful things.

Beauty begins within.

I am a beautiful girl.

Beautiful Girl Challenge

Share with the world just how beautiful you are!
Here's how:

Post a video or picture of you

#1 - Saying something Beautiful
#2 - Doing something Beautiful
#3 - Being Beautiful

Join the #BeautifulGirlChallenge today!

Hashtags

#BeautifulGirlChallenge
#BGChallenge

About the Author

Ciara Ijames is a multi-award-winning author and poet. Her works as a poet and author range from children's books to adult poetry collections. She currently resides in Ohio where she writes books helping girls around the world see their beauty.

Follow Me

Find Ciara Ijames talking about her books and other good stuff on your favorite app!

 @Ciaraijames

www.ingramcontent.com/pod-product-compliance
Lightning Source LLC
Chambersburg PA
CBHW041439010526
44118CB00002B/128